Six Doors to the Seventh Dimension

Six Doors *to the* Seventh Dimension

Timothy Carson
Genevieve A. Howard
Jenny McGee

WIPF & STOCK · Eugene, Oregon

SIX DOORS TO THE SEVENTH DIMENSION

Copyright © 2014 Timothy Carson, Genevieve A. Howard, and Jenny McGee. All rights reserved. Except for brief quotations in critical publications or reviews, no part of this book may be reproduced in any manner without prior written permission from the publisher. Write: Permissions. Wipf and Stock Publishers, 199 W. 8th Ave., Suite 3, Eugene, OR 97401.

Wipf and Stock
An Imprint of Wipf and Stock Publishers
199 W. 8th Ave., Suite 3
Eugene, OR 97401

www.wipfandstock.com

ISBN 13: 978-1-62564-532-6

Manufactured in the U.S.A.   07/08/2014

We dedicate this book to our families
and to those who strive to create homes of peace and joy
everywhere.

Contents

Preface | ix
Acknowledgments | xv

House Plans | 1

Chapter 1
Back Door | 7

Chapter 2
Side Door Left | 15

Chapter 3
Side Door Right | 23

Chapter 4
Front Door | 31

Chapter 5
Basement Door | 41

Chapter 6
Attic Door | 49

The Seventh Dimension | 57

About the Creators | 63

Preface

The creation of this book came about through the collaboration of three persons—Tim Carson, Jenny McGee, and Genevieve Howard. The end product is the result of walking together in creative freedom. From the beginning, we recognized that the book would be completed by you, the reader, as you imagine a world out in front of our words and images on the printed page. And so we would like to introduce ourselves and share some of the process that unfolded on the way to this moment.

Tim

In our community of Columbia, Missouri, the art league had just completed a creative exposition in which writers and visual artists were paired to interpret one another's work. Many of these cross-interpretations were astounding, picking up on spoken and unspoken beauty, energy, and insights of the creative partners. This collaborative model was fresh in our minds as Jenny, Genevieve, and I became excited about the potential and promise of the *Six Doors* concept. The more we explored the possibilities, the more convinced we became that the flourishing of *Six Doors* would also depend on a creative collaboration. Though the search for partners had not been difficult, this would be the first time we had worked together on such a project. We all became enthused immediately.

But how would we proceed? We devised a process that included both structure and maximum freedom. That kind of an

Preface

approach required a high level of trust, something we already held for one another. For each section of the book we would follow the same steps: I would provide the narrative to Jenny, she would create an original work of art based on her response, Genevieve would receive my narrative and Jenny's art at once, as a reader might, and then respond with a reflective work of prose-poetry. All this we did without explaining or interpreting our portion to the other partners in advance in order to safeguard the creative response of each. We moved through the house door by door, using this method as we went. It was an adventure of discovery and creativity.

As for my portion, creating the narrative, I spent much time envisioning the house, its doors, and what existed behind them. I had some idea of what to bring to each conceptual dimension, but I also discovered new aspects and connections behind the doors as they opened in the imagination. Throughout the story I maintain the first-person voice of a narrator-guide, directly addressing the reader. To assist in my visualization, I constructed a simple schematic model of a six-sided house. It became very helpful in my contemplation, especially when I seemed to get stuck. As I composed the narrative, I attempted to follow a certain discipline, that of avoiding explicitly religious language. It is far too easy to rely on inherited insider code language when describing the deepest realities of life. Such language is often baffling to those who are not familiar with it and misunderstood by those who are. So instead we let the story tell the truths in its own way.

Jenny

One of the reasons I became so excited about this project is that none of us were interested in a collection of illustrations to amplify the printed words. I desired something far greater than that, a way for the original art to serve as a visual co-author throughout the book. I wanted to tell my side of the story through my hands, black ink and emotions. Let me share some of how I did that.

In the course of the process it was important for me not to judge the image or critique its visual form too harshly. I trusted enough to leap and then trust that a net would appear. Leaping is what I did after reading each chapter: I sat and focused on the emotions and feelings Tim's narrative evoked. Then I dipped a cotton string into ink and started exploring the movements of my hand in response to the emotions stirring inside me. I used three simple tools - ink, string, and paper. This seemed like the appropriate amount of material to convey and interpret this internal emotional dialogue. I decided when the image was complete by trusting my gut reaction. I intuitively knew when it was time to pass it on to Genevieve so she could begin her excursus.

Genevieve

I suffer from the typical 21st century condition of the over-busy woman: always pulled between my roles as mom, wife, employee, family member, friend, volunteer, and pony owner. Most any other potential project at this point in my life would have yielded the same response; I would have said no. But the opportunity to work with Tim as narrator and Jenny as artist was impossible to pass up. I knew that our collaborative work would be potent and nourishing, each of us building off of and learning from one another. It would be like playing a game of creativity tag.

I approached this project as a devotional practice. So that you might understand how that practice informed the way I wrote, let me describe the way I worked in a typical session. Let's pretend you are right there with me:

I change into comfortable clothes, get myself a hot drink, and light a candle. I find a relaxed position so nothing constricts me. I take a deep breath. My self-awareness is usually centered in my head. I do a quick visualization to reconnect me to my body. I envision a silver thread of heaven at the top of my head. Moving my awareness down, a pink glow from my heart goes out to my arms and fingers. I imagine love flowing through to my pen. I take a deep breath in my belly, the source of power. I feel warmth in my diaphragm as if an orange sun is shining. In the bowl of my pelvis, I picture it like a basket I can settle myself in. I bring my awareness lower into my legs and feet. I wiggle my toes. I imagine they turn into roots deep in the earth.

I welcome the gentle rain of grace. I imagine it rinsing away the accumulation of the day: stresses, misunderstandings, and disappointments. Grace covers me, cleans me, and clarifies my thoughts. I say a blessing: *God bless my hands to write your words, bless my mind to know your mind, bless my heart to beat in your rhythm.* I am refreshed and ready to write.

Then I sit with the piece. I spend time listening. With Jenny's art, I follow the lines of ink. With Tim's pieces, I read them line by line, savoring the language and experience of mentally traveling through the rooms. I use a journal and my favorite fat pen because I intentionally decided to do this project in longhand so my tools would slow me down.

The process depends on the day; sometimes it's a fulfilling flow. Other times, I feel stalled out. I keep with it, if only to write, *I don't know what to write.* I practice the art of noticing. As the images come, I write them all down, positive or negative, embarrassing or confusing.

I trust the fragments. Later I impose structure and syntax on my work so it makes enough sense for others to follow. But the creative process is loose, fluid, and open.

* * *

The contributors to this book write and create through a certain lens of faith; we are self-identified Christians. That worldview and those shared convictions do indeed shape our perspectives. For us the ever present and creating Spirit is known in particular through Jesus. Even so, we recognize that the sacred reality is present in all times and places. For that reason we hope that our work is sufficiently broad and open to speak to the hearts of all people.

Some will describe this book as a religious work, an apologetic, a different way to make the case for Christian faith to our culture. Others may view it as a philosophical parable. A few persons will read it as a psychological view of the human being, a type of anthropology. Those schooled in mystical movements and writers may notice the time-honored use of geography or space to speak metaphorically of spiritual matters: Dante's *Divine Comedy*, St. Teresa of Avila's *Interior Castle*, Thomas Merton's *Seven Story Mountain*, or René Daumal's *Mount Analogue*. One cannot imagine Harry Potter's famed Hogwarts School without at the same time finding multiple layers of meaning hidden in those rooms, chambers, corridors, and passageways.

To be sure, the curious reader may discover any or all of the above-mentioned aspects, at least to some degree. But most of all, we want to tell a story. And we hope you will find yourself in it.

Acknowledgments

From the very beginning of this project we enjoyed the generous support of our families, and we thank them for their love and encouragement. The staff of *Wipf & Stock Publishing* has been sure and stellar; they believed in our idea and walked with us toward its fulfillment. None of our efforts could have shone as clearly without the careful and tireless copyediting of Nancy Miller. For all our friends and colleagues who told us in as many words, "Go for it!" we offer our deep appreciation. The best things in life come when we are surrounded by those who love us. Most of all, we are filled with wonder at the many sources of inspiration, both human and divine, that endlessly make themselves known to us.

House Plans

Welcome! I have been waiting for you. Your journey has been so very long and difficult. Won't you come in off the porch and make yourself at home? Let me take your coat and bag, and you can freshen up before we have a bite to eat to soften that hunger. Please make yourself at home right here by the fire, and I will throw another log on.

I remember, back when you first made your reservation, just how hesitant you were. It is a scary thing to make this kind of decision, I know. You were so nervous. But you have to know that almost everyone who comes here has the same reaction. So don't worry. The important thing is that you *are* here. That's what matters now.

The first thing to know, before we go on a tour of the house, is that nothing in this place is accidental. Each facet of the house has a purpose, each room plays a special role, and every door leads somewhere in particular. So the most important place to begin is with your own attention, your willingness to see what's in front of you. As your guide, I will do my very best to assist, but it is impossible for me to help without your willingness. You might be surprised how many people turn away when they find themselves standing at the edge of their own greatest opportunity. I am hoping the best for you.

Along the way there will be moments when you are tempted to stop. That is perfectly normal. Our old attachments are persistent. What you find may be so frightening or unpleasant that you want to avoid it. But don't worry. You will have all the time in the world to deal with each thing as it comes. This is not a timed tour. And if it ever seems too much, too fast, the chair in front of the fireplace will be waiting. Consider it your island of safety.

Now for a little orientation before we begin our walk. This house has been around forever. Everyone ever born receives an invitation to this tour. Most people are surprised when the invitation comes, and they respond just like you did. Others pass and never come. And no one is ever forced to come here against their will, not even the slightest coercion. You arrive at this place by one way only, through your own choice, an act of your own free will. Each and every person is invited, but the decision as to how to respond belongs to that individual alone. So some of the story is determined, like the opportunity and the tour, but some of it you create out of your own freedom.

Did you happen to see the house even before you arrived, perhaps in your dreams or through some painting? If so, you are in good company, for many have that same experience. It doesn't seem to matter where they live or how they grew up; the same house they imagined all those years is exactly the one they find. Many features of the house are identical for everybody because people are the same in so many ways. The differences—furnishings, arrangements, contents—have to do with what is distinctive about your particular life. Remember, everything here has a purpose and a reason for being just as it is.

Now that you are inside the house, you may see things you didn't notice when you stood on the outside. If you think you see a hidden geometric pattern, you are not imagining it; there is one. The house is a six-sided cube and each of the six sides has a door. Each one of these six doors reveals a threshold through which you must pass to see what you must see. Our tour will take you to one door and threshold at a time, but first we need to get acquainted with the inside of the house.

Right now you are standing in the center of the main floor. This entire floor represents your life as it is lived in real time, your ordinary, everyday existence. This is where you take care of business. From this vantage point you look out on the world and try to make sense of it. And as we move from room to room, you will notice the needs, preoccupations, and habits that constitute your daily life. Without some of them you could scarcely live, or at least not for long. Others make life more comfortable and pleasurable. And some make it harder than it needs to be, for one reason or another.

Let's begin with the room we are in right now, the living room. You will notice the most obvious things first: shelter, protection, and a roof over your head. It is also a place to gather socially, receive guests, extend hospitality, and spend time with loved ones. The other rooms on this floor are just as familiar to you.

Over there is the kitchen, made to keep, prepare, and serve the food you need. You clean up in the sink and retrieve your water through the faucet. Just across from the refrigerator is an island for food preparation. When you awaken, your coffee maker is waiting for you on the short counter by the microwave. The pantry with the long, vertical doors holds all your non-perishables. The stove sits nestled among cabinets that hold pots and pans, dishes and glasses, and the trash can rests under the sink. The kitchen is one of the most essential places in the house, the place where you provide for eating and drinking. And it connects to the dining room where you and your guests eat what you made.

On the way down the center hallway, we pass the laundry room where you clean your clothes, and then the bathroom where you clean yourself. You are a creature who needs a toilet just as much as a dining table, a simple fact. You spend more or less time in front of the mirror, depending on what you deem necessary or what vanity requires. The tub and shower wash off each day's portion of grime and help you along toward being presentable to the rest of your tribe.

At the end of the hallway is your bedroom, your womb for sleep and den for sex when you do have sex. Some of your best times can be here, the place where rest comes and sleep restores. Pictures on the wall remind you of those you love or who went before you. If you share your bed with someone you love, it may also be a place of intimacy, play, and delight. Your closets and bureaus hold your clothing, shoes, hats, scarves, and bangles. This is where you appoint yourself against the cold, the heat, the rain and snow. It is also a place to adorn yourself to move among others as you wish them to see you.

These are the rooms of your daily life, divided and combined on the main floor of the six-sided house. Many things transpire within these walls. The television brings in a world of shows, news, and opinion. Your electronic devices follow you from room to room like a virtual puppy dog. An inordinate amount of your pastime conversation with others revolves around these very things.

As time passes, the pursuit and securing of these daily essentials may begin to wear on you. This is not because you are ungrateful or would choose to do without them. No, the source of your discontentment is found elsewhere. If you look down inside your uneasiness, it has to do with the repeating, everyday nature of things. Don't worry; everyone has experienced that at one time or another. It's just that some people address it and others don't. The ones who don't slowly dial down their expectations in order to adjust to the increasing flatness. They resign themselves to living a two-dimensional life.

When that time comes, and it will, your first response may be to ward off the rising awareness that tomorrow is going to be just like yesterday and the day before. That is what we all dread, and you will, too. When we come to the point where we don't know whether we can endure one more conversation about the day's routines, one more night of television or video games or surfing Facebook, we may become motivated to make a change. When you get there, you will know it. If you are limited to this floor, this dimension of life, you will soon long to outgrow it.

Are you ready for a tour of the doors yet? If so, come with me.

Excursus

For me, the house comes from dreams. Every house should provide protection. Yet I sense this dwelling is different: it offers renewal. It restores broken connections. As an outsider, I felt depressed, discouraged. Then I was welcomed inside. How warm is a friendly hearth after the cold! What a comfort I won't be alone! It would be hard to wander around in this house on my own.

I hesitated when I first heard about the tour. I was curious but unsure. Sometimes it seems there is something others have, know, or understand. But not me. Now it's me. Now I'm here. I'm nervous, but the good kind of nervous. Like a first ride without training wheels, I have to be willing to scrape my knee.

After we went through the main floor set of rooms, I realized I know this level of life too well. It's the world of humdrum everyday noise: mumbling from a TV and random notification buzzes. It's the speed of cars and digital devices. I long to come back to my feet. To come back to breath.

I imagine myself as a dragonfly, a creature from ancient days, clinging to a stalk among tall growing wildflowers and grasses. I hold tight before an exhilarating wind catches me to whoosh me up. For this moment, I rest and sway with the stem. I gather strength before taking flight.

I keep my heart too tightly wound. I need to trust in this process and let the patterns take shape, as an artist guides the ink; but the ink has its own desires. It wants to meet the paper, stain the fibers. The fibers reflect on how sunshine hit the leaves. They remember.

If I stay with the house, I'll learn from the timbers. Rooms will reveal what I need to know. I'm ready to concentrate, to live a rich and consecrated life. Who will I be at the end of this? The tour will open doors for me. I'm ready to experience them.

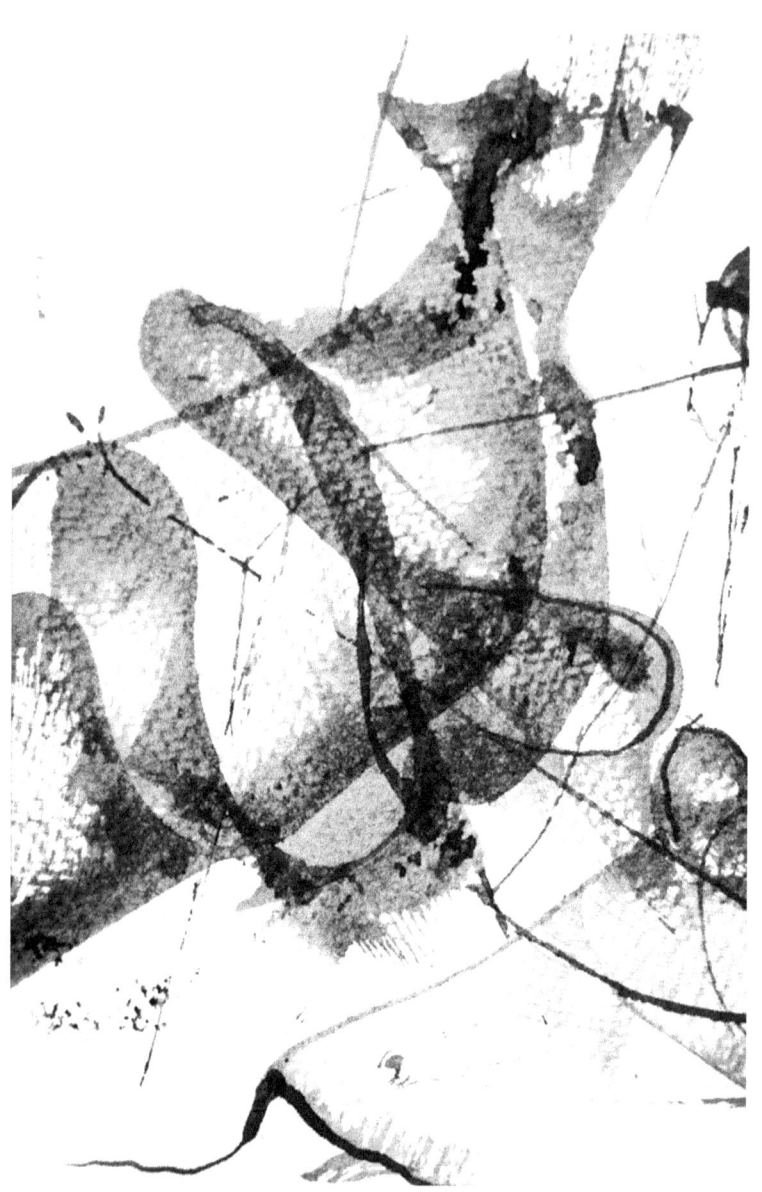

Chapter 1

Back Door

Every door does at least two things: it reveals and conceals. A door fits in the opening between here and there, protecting and separating us from what is on the other side. As it covers, it also obscures, blocking what can be seen. But the same door that keeps things out can also let them in, if you open it, that is. That is the way a door works. Every door in this house acts exactly that way.

You may wonder why I am bringing you to the back door first. There are two reasons, really. The first is that the back door is often the real front door. That is where your friends enter and the kids pile out from the car parked in the drive by the garage. You bring in the groceries through this door and pass through to the kitchen. The back door is the familiar door where people you know enter when they visit. So this is a good place to begin, with the familiar door.

The second reason is more important. We are approaching this door first because it is the door to your past. When you pass through this threshold, it is to what has been already been. In fact, it is the door to the entire past of everyone. And this is the first essential stop on our tour of the house.

Lots of people get nervous standing here. Most of the time they try to keep this door locked tight. But it somehow keeps opening all by itself without permission. Sometimes you walk into the room and find it standing ajar. People sometimes attribute this to intruders, but that is not the case. The truth is that you cannot batten down the hatches of the past; it is alive and well and brings forward everything, including you, to right now.

When you are ready, take a deep breath, turn the doorknob, and open the door.

If you look outside the door, you will see a pathway that seems hazier the farther you gaze into the distance. That is because our most recent memories usually stand out most vividly. The more distant our experience, the more phantom-like it appears. Regardless of how short-term or long-term the memories, they all are based in our experience. But we only know part of them and even the part recalled is remembered through the emotions of the time and the way we wanted the story to be. Ask anyone else who was present for the same event, and their recitation of events may seem very different. The past is always seen through a particular set of eyes and filtered through a certain lens. It belongs to everyone but is remembered uniquely.

Like the ocean, the tide of the past keeps washing up debris on the shore of the present. We walk on its artifacts, trash, and creatures all the time. The more willing we are to keep the back door to the past open, the more we become like beachcombers. We are not dominated by the past but rather become anthropologists of time. We retrieve the signs of the past with curiosity, asking questions of them, how they shaped us and shape us still.

Some of the memories are still sharp, with jagged edges. They are unpleasant to hold and cause our hands to bleed when we pick them up. These are the memories that keep shredding us even when we try to forget them, and hurt us when we finally pluck them off the shore. They comprise a menagerie of our lost loves, failures, moral indiscretions, disappointments, hurts, violations, and trauma. These shards of the past are often slow to heal. They never take their place easily or gracefully. But, like every other thing, the sharp edges of our past eventually wear off, as do mountain tops and the teeth of saws.

Healing the past is hard emotional and spiritual work. Our painful memories live in us, in every cell of every organ in our whole body. And because of that, every cell of our body is also an access point of healing. We are living repositories enveloped by spirit and energy. Even the most horrendous moments may be healed by an even more transforming spirit of love and acceptance. We stand on the shore holding the notorious thing in our own hands, but *we are holding it*. The tragedy, the loss, the insult or yes, even the unspeakable inhumanity, is held in no other hands than our own in this very moment. It *is* possible to transform the past in this moment, in this heart. I know that may not seem possible to you right now, but I never would have invited you to open the door in the first place if it were not.

Of course, our shoreline is also littered with glittering treasures of joy, richness, triumph, belonging, love, and hopes realized. How could we have possibly been the recipients of such beauty, opportunity, richness, and grace? But it's true, we have been. We have been enfolded by the light, power, and mystery of life we have called God. We bend over and pick these treasures up with gentle hands, turning them over and over, feeling their distinctive texture, smiling as we relive them. Some blessings came to us late, or seemed to come late. Many were placed on our doorsteps by the love of those around us, disclosed through sensitive souls. And the very best seem to have just appeared out of nowhere, unearned and unsought. They just *were*. We would have never been the same without them, whether enjoyed for a season or a lifetime. Say thank you. Say it twice.

This is the biography of your life, the tragedy, comedy, and wonder of it. It cannot be rewritten. But it can be redeemed in the present. The way we receive it and what we do with it shapes the story. If we take blessings for granted, stroll through our days chewing on our bitterness, or simply give up because we anticipate more of the same, then the past has one flavor. If, on the other hand, we understand the past as flowing into a new vision, then the past is made different by virtue of how its story ends.

Six Doors to the Seventh Dimension

Now the hard or joyful work begins. If you take courage, refuse to flee, and instead face what shows itself, you may claim your transformed life. In order to do so, certain practices are necessary, practices that are absolutely essential for navigating the other side of the door. Now spend time with each one:

Allow gratitude to redefine your past.
Seek forgiveness.
Extend forgiveness.
Learn from what was.
Claim your whole story.
Know that though the past may not be re-lived,
it may be granted new meaning
by the way the end of the story
is written in the present.

This is the spiritual assignment on the other side of the back door. But it does not end there.

If the past could be understood by means of only a personal history, then coming to terms with it would be fairly simple, however difficult. But it is not only the product of our personal history. We are a part of a massive collective past that extends infinitely, to a time long before our birth, before the birth of anyone we know or can remember, beyond the rise of our species, the formation of this planet, the unfolding of our galaxy and all galaxies, the inception of the universe and its genesis. Our personal past is a part of a massive past, and it rolls to our shore with much, much more than the ripples of our individual experience.

Of course, just the thought of that leaves us whirling in something so big we cannot comprehend it. But we should never reduce the scope of the universe to our ability to comprehend it; that would be much too small. The reason we feel so small is a good one; it is because we *are* so small. As strange as it may seem at first, that awareness of smallness is a good thing, a very good thing. Drawing ourselves into that majestic scope puts everything in its right perspective.

It's not just me, but everybody. It's not just everybody, but everybody everywhere. It's not just everybody everywhere, but all those throughout all time. It's beyond everybody everywhere throughout all time. It's every cellular creature that ever lived from the beginning.

That is incomprehensibly dense and big. And that is exactly how you should see yourself: no less than a part of it all, but no more either; neither diminished nor grandiose.

Opening the back door to the past and walking through it is humbling business. But it connects us to everything that has already been in just the right way. Now you can rest. You are responsible for your life, but not for everything. It is a delusion to believe that everything rises or falls on what we do or did. Even so, our life and actions do matter. We are only molecules of a whale swimming the Milky Way. But we *are* those molecules.

When you are ready, follow me to the next door. Feel free to rest in your special chair on the way. This is hard work.

Excursus

The umbilical cord is cut, but the belly always remembers.

A baby puts her arms up, hands out, reaches with expectation. Bad things happen. She stops reaching. She keeps her arms clamped to her side. Stiffness settles in the shoulders. The ground pulls the arms down. Arms—made for raising—flop, drained of strength.

I'm one of those people who tried to close the door to the past, but it wouldn't stay shut. I wanted to blot out what was behind this door. Even the joyful moments seemed bleak, because they were over. Remembering laughter reminded me I wasn't laughing.

I couldn't make sense of the smeared memories and sadness, the pains and pleasures scrambled. I was caught in a cruel trap of thoughts. The more I struggled, the tighter the past held me. It tore into my mind.

I held a lungful of air a long time. Then I realized I wasn't under water. I could breathe. I let my shoulders drop. I felt the joints glide.

I raise my arms in welcome to the past, with its starfish and sharp shells, its seaweed and sea foam. How could it hurt me now? I observe it with the eyes of a survivor. I can tell my story of traveling the seas with the confidence of standing on the shore.

"Seek forgiveness. Extend forgiveness. Learn from what was." I misunderstood the velvet folds of my days remembered. I described them as difficult to see through, too heavy, opaque. Yet they were never meant to be seen through, but felt. They can be beautiful to touch, soft to the finger like petting a mole, fragile mammal bones under a plush exterior. Let us remember how we were tender and small. The belly remembers.

I'm here now.

I'm happy to be a single stitch on a quilt of stars, sand, and ash. Stitches run along either side of me, and in some rare and graceful moments, I'm not a stitch, but part of a thread.

How good to be small, a piece and not the whole, a part and not the center.

Chapter 2

Side Door Left

This is one of two doors in the house that has windows. As you can see, this door looks out into the deep woods. These trees stand on land that is pristine and undeveloped. Day after day you may hear the sounds of wildlife. Birds sing and deer appear at the edge of the forest without warning. Your yard merges with the rest of the natural world beyond your yard.

This door has windows so that every time you pass by you will remember that what is on the inside of the house and what is on the outside are integrally connected. When you open the door and pass through the threshold to the side porch, you are also standing on nature's porch. If you turn around and look back toward the house, you realize that the porch is really a bridge going both ways, depending upon what direction you face at the moment. Call it the house's porch or nature's porch; it really doesn't matter because it is both.

When you are ready, take a deep breath, turn the doorknob, and open the door.

We two-legged, big-brained creatures have crashed nature's ongoing party. When we are at our best, we live in harmony with nature and assume special responsibility for its care. And the way we tend this relationship with our larger natural world sets the stage for our flourishing or decay. Nature's destiny is our own.

Much of our human dis-ease comes from a case of amnesia, forgetting that before we were here, before houses held people or people built houses, nature *was*. We have become estranged from the body that gave us birth, the larger natural world. The more our lives have become anchored in cities of stone and steel, glass and plastic, the more anxious and unhealthy we have become. We have become anxious because the artificial and temporary world we have created is one estranged from its source. We have become unhealthy because we have physically lost contact with the natural healing forces of the earth. In our more thoughtful moments, we have the deep-down suspicion that something has gone terribly wrong in our relationship with nature. And we are right.

If you hike over the next ridge, you will discover a beautiful and tranquil lake. The Blue Herons glide through the twilight and stand motionless in the shallows. The surface of the green water reflects all that is above it, inviting the moon to join the evening solitude. When you sit still, very still, it is possible to hear not only your own pulse, but the pulse of the world.

This tranquility is often short-lived. By midday, deafening speed boats crash across the watery landscape, drowning out every sound other than the grind of their own engines. They are not making an appearance for an important race. This is not a test run before competition. No, this is a human attempt to dominate nature by machine, to exercise more power than is necessary, to sully what is beautiful with what enlarges ego. The noise of the motor erects yet another wall of separation between guest and host, the human creature wearing out its welcome. This imposition on nature has become our repeating story, one that insures our self-isolation.

As long as we define ourselves in terms of domination, we undermine our tenuous place within the web of life. Our hubris is not only destined to fail, but also to leave us exhausted and alone. The only way forward toward a harmonious and sustainable future involves balance and partnership. We must ride the waves rather than contend with them. We must become the waves rather than manage them. We must dive beneath the waves rather than resist them.

What the door to the forest requires of us is what it always has—a respect for the creation that gives us birth and sustains us. The ancient wisdom of the great religious traditions has always known this: the sacred is to be found in the natural, ordinary, material world and reverence for creation leads to a profound stewardship of what has been received. We walk lightly on that which is not ours to possess, harm, or defile. And this reverence for all creation will manifest itself in a remarkable compassion for all creatures.

We are not sentimental when it comes to the power of nature, the ways in which our species is harmed by being in the wrong place at the wrong time. The natural world of which we are a part is beautiful in ways that leave us speechless. But it may also overtake and crush us with its unwieldy force. This is not personal, some intention of the creator that some perish and others survive before gale winds, shaking earth, or crashing waters. No, those are simply the natural changes and shifts in the earth's becoming. When we are affected by them in cataclysmic ways, it may seem personal, as though directed at us. But the world does not revolve around us. In fact, as regards us, nature is impersonal in its moving, not noticing our coming and going. At the same time, we are very dependent upon it.

The natural world is also the source of much of our healing and well-being. It holds healing properties in its plants and herbs. Our communion with its force and beauty restores our balance. When our perspective becomes too small or self-centered, a walk through the forest, swim in the ocean, or view from the mountain restores our perspective. Distance and separation from the natural world brings the opposite result, a diminished life in which we feel cut off from our source.

In a very direct sense, our physical contact with the natural world, our body in contact with the earth's body, allows for healing and well-being. We know this not only from our own experience and from the testimony of spiritual traditions throughout the millennia, but from current science. The earth encompasses a huge field of energy that is itself set in a larger cosmos of energy. The free electrons pulsing through its crust into our own body's field of energy resets us and promotes healing, well-being, and the reduction of pain.

Is it any wonder why so many of the great spiritual traditions express the principle of going barefoot before the holiness of the universe? Take off your shoes: you stand on holy ground. Walk lightly on the earth, for it is sacred. Feel rooted to the earth beneath your feet.

Our estrangement from the natural world requires a process of reconciliation that is both mental and physical. The first requires a re-enchantment of the world and our place within it; our attitude toward our planet must move from dominance to reverence. The second is very practical and involves our bodies. To re-establish a right relationship, we must place ourselves in intimate contact with all the manifestations of the natural world. This means actually touching, walking through, sitting on, swimming in, and breathing its life-giving energy. Take off your shoes.

Now the hard or joyful work begins. If you take courage, refuse to flee, and instead face what shows itself, you may claim your transformed life. In order to do so, certain practices are necessary, practices that are absolutely essential for navigating the other side of the door. Now spend time with each one:

> Allow wonder to redefine your relationship with nature.
> Commit to protecting the garden of nature.
> Turn to nature for the healing of body, mind, and spirit.
> Unite your life cycle with the earth's cycle of days, months, and years.
> Learn from the wisdom of other species.
> Value nature as an end in itself and not only a means to benefit humans.
> Celebrate that which is bigger than you, that to which you belong.
> Go barefoot, lie in the grass, climb a tree, swim in the ocean.

This is a door you must walk through often. Call your mind and body into stillness before nature's grandeur and majesty. Dare to feel small and temporary before the trees and mountains, rocks and valleys that preceded you and will outlast you. Only then will you see yourself rightly, placing the brief moment that is your life before the everlasting moments of the whole earth, galaxy, universe, and cosmos. You are precious and gifted, possessing a mind that knows it belongs and is able to merge into life's spacious backdrop and become one with it.

When you are ready, follow me to the next door. Feel free to rest in your special chair on the way. This is hard work.

Excursus

Nature's porch. The idea that the porch belongs to the outside world as much as to the house made me stop and think.

Urban chaos with its straight lines and tense ideas of ownership blends into curves and communal life on nature's porch. Picture a tree, strong beside blurry water. Who owns the branch—the tree or the bird perched on it? The wind that moves it, or the sun that lights up its leaves?

Ah, our sun, the star of our every day. In winter, I miss the sun. I long to realign my body to the rhythm of sun and moon, winter and summer. Immersed in the artificial, I live under electric lights, sometimes in the office from dawn to dusk. The closest nature is a house plant and landscape photos on a computer screen. The true life calls: hearty, guttural, and breathy.

Nature can seem severe to us creatures with hairless soft skin, but "the world does not revolve around us." How liberating to not be in charge of the world's revolution, the storms and earthquakes, the rains and the wind! How would we ever agree on how the world should revolve? We might have whole days with the planet stopped.

I can let nature be big and I will stay small. I will go to the water and see the sun rise in two places: above and across, sky and reflection.

I'll be a windsurfer, no engine to chew up the lake, only my sail puffed out as I glide on. The blue herons on the shore won't be bothered by me. I will see animals with new eyes, natural eyes to replace the harsh eyes of a superior.

I imagine how life must be for a snake, its belly streaming along the soil, always in contact, always supported. It lives on the earth with its whole body. We touch the earth with the few inches of our feet, and those are usually covered in shoes.

Side Door Left

I'm ready for another walk outside. My toes will make friends with soft green grass blades.

Chapter 3

Side Door Right

This is the other door in the house that has windows. Like the door of nature, this door allows you to see out every time you pass by it. It also has a porch that connects to what is beyond. What you find outside this door is your human neighborhood, those in your tribe and other tribes.

All those other houses also hold two-legged, big-brained neighbors, a neighborhood of houses, a cluster of neighborhoods, a hive of clusters, a group of hives, a region of groups, a continent of regions, a planet of continents. And all of these creatures, regardless of their superficial differences, cultural distinctiveness, and national identities, have virtually the same code of DNA determining almost all of who they are. The differences are negligible.

When you are ready, take a deep breath, turn the doorknob, and open the door.

Almost all the religious traditions of the world have some teaching that parallels the Golden Rule, a principle that insists you treat your neighbor as you hope you get treated. This is the high measuring stick of love. Whether love is actualized as the result of a high humanitarian impulse or the most self-interested one, doing the loving thing is of supreme importance. Our self-interest is always tied to the common good. The very existence of such a principle, however, reminds us that we don't do it very well; we often fail and find ourselves contending with people as much as cooperating with them. That is not new among the two-legged, big-brained ones.

Our species competes for resources and contends for power. This is primarily driven by our survival instinct and is one of the reasons we survived when other groups did not. But we have also stayed alive through cooperation, by combining resources to overcome threats. Now, more than ever, our collaborating will insure our greatest chance of survival. The challenges are too great to overcome otherwise. This will require attention to the needs of the many as well as the achievements of the one.

Like the Biblical story in which the animals go into Noah's ark in pairs, the most primary unit of human relationship is one-to-one. Because binary relationships are so very primary, their success or failure often portends all other successes and failures. Every conflict finds its origin in the failures of the one-to-one pairings of individuals, families, tribes, and nations. Wherever fear, aggression, pride, greed, and selfishness predominate, human relationships are fractured. And only the powers of forgiveness, solidarity, mutual companionship, and common cause allow for their healing.

Some of the greatest suffering in your life has come with the breaking of relationships, very often the ones closest and most important to you. Our villages and tribes exist to protect and provide, but they also may confine and control. Our marriages exist to nurture, create, and encourage, but they also may empty and hurt. Our families exist to shape, enfold, and comfort, but they also may alienate and sadden. All of these relationships provide the best and worst. Opening the door to loving our neighbor is at once the most important and seemingly impossible thing we can do. We are social creatures at the core, but our social nature is often unfulfilled, even the source of suffering.

Each person experiences more richness in some parts of the social web than in others. I may find immense pleasure with a select few friends, but do not fare as well when it comes to the tribal meal of twenty-five. I may be the life of the party, but have difficulty in establishing deep intimacy or commitment with one person. My sense of belonging to my tribe or nation may be strong while I feel cut off from the larger global community. I may understand the intricacies of subtle political maneuvering, but be oblivious to the dynamics of my own family. Our access to different parts of the social web is uneven and our relational growth challenges different.

In the same way that suffering comes from broken relationships, so our healing comes with their repairing. In fact, the restoration of right relationships makes healing and flourishing possible. Whenever more than two people are in the room, love must take the form of justice. That means that right relationships extend into family, tribe, groups, nations, and world. And until justice is established through right relationships, love cannot be said to really exist, for love is more than a feeling; love is securing the best good for the neighbor. And love is the first and last word at the core of our communal existence.

Love is the rare, beautiful, and healing power that transcends the walls and fences we construct for self-protection. We attempt to protect ourselves from perceived and real threats, and also safeguard a sense of our identity. Because many of these walls are fear-based, only love will find a way to transcend them and open them. Once we restore broken relationships, the walls of estrangement become irrelevant barriers, artifacts of brokenness.

Love asks something of us and often stretches us toward self-sacrifice. The great moral figures throughout history have demonstrated this willingness to give of oneself even when personal pleasure or security is diminished. This is why other-giving love is not sentimental and is more than either attachment or desire of the object of attraction. In fact, there is no love greater than this: that a person lay down his or her life for the sake of the other. It at once benefits the neighbor and frees us from excessive self-centeredness.

Now the hard or joyful work begins. If you take courage, refuse to flee, and instead face what shows itself, you may claim your transformed life. In order to do so, certain practices are necessary, practices that are absolutely essential for navigating the other side of the door. Now spend time with each one:

Six Doors to the Seventh Dimension

> Allow love to redefine your web of relationships.
> Give thanks for those you love one-by-one.
> Attempt to reconcile with one from whom you are estranged.
> Venture something selfless in a struggling relationship.
> Serve as a bridge-builder between groups in conflict.
> Seek a mutually beneficial solution for a future of peace.
> Pursue justice as the way to love the many.
> Follow the demand of love even when it requires much.

For us two-legged, big-brained creatures, most of our existence is lived out in a social web; it defines who we are. More than what we earn, buy, or possess, our relationships are our most important commodity. I am because you are, and you are because I am.

Living in community balances our strengths with the unique strengths of others. When we are together, we become more than what we could be without the other. What we create alone may abundantly enrich the many. But right relationship—characterized by mutual love, justice, and common purpose—transforms the individual, tribe, and community of tribes.

There is one more thing to notice: When you stand in the center of the house with the left-side door to nature open and the right-side door to humanity open, you have a clear view all the way through both doors. Glancing left to right, you have a clear line of sight between nature and humanity. That's not an accident, because they are meant to coexist and balance one another.

When you are ready, follow me to the next door. Feel free to rest in your special chair on the way. This is hard work.

Excursus

Our first dance is at the breast of our mother. We learn to ask and to drink from her body. She learns to hold us and give from her very bones. This first flow between people sets up how we learn to give and take, to trust or pull back. If our early experiences left us thirsty and sad, healing is possible. Healing is always possible.

Healing comes through reaching out. Where we reached out in wanting as children, now we reach out with offerings as adults. We can be angels of service, arms wide, serving platters full of food for those who are hungry.

Inside each person is a seed pod. The seeds can take root and grow toward our neighbor, or they can stay small and stunted.

We choose the depth of love we walk in. Our soil might be rich, dark. and vital. We shed our old resentments like leaves. They fall to the ground in a thick carpet, adding organic matter and richness to our interactions. We understand other viewpoints. We stay connected.

If we've been rejected too many times and only see parties from a distance, our depth of love might be shallow sand, gritty in our eyes and abrasive on our skin. Loneliness can make us brutal. Hot from winds of anger, we might flare up and protect ourselves with sharp words like spears.

I know what it is to live without love, to be alone in the desert, without shelter or friend. I know what it is to wear spikes and build walls as protection. Yet the way without love is a slow way of dying. Without others, we cannot thrive.

I'm willing to choose love, the healing power that flows over all walls no matter their height, no matter how many spirals of razor wire.

Six Doors to the Seventh Dimension

    Love is the welcome drink to a soul behind barriers spiky as a cactus. We will serve that drink and carry our tray to those who can't or won't meet us in the middle. Let us go farther and give the very bones of us to transformation.

Chapter 4

Front Door

The front door opens into the future, what will be, and for that reason it has no windows. We cannot gaze into that which has not yet happened. But just because we do not know what is coming next, the future in no way slows its march toward us. In every moment the future of *not-yet* is colliding with the present of *what-is*. Just as quickly, the present of *what-is* is passing into the past of *what-was*. The present is a fleeting sliver compared to either the potential of the future or the history log of the past. And yet everything actually takes place in the present moment without exception. The present reveals what used to be the future. And it creates what will become the past.

When you are ready, take a deep breath, turn the doorknob, and open the door.

Some people say that the answer to life's predicaments is found in the past; it sets the stage and determines what is yet to come, providing wisdom and perspective. Others remind us that the present is the primary time in which everything happens, the moment in which we act and things change: if you are going to focus anywhere, let it be on the present. Both of these are true. The main floor of the present and back door of the past are essential aspects of the house of your life. But they are not the only ones. There is also the future.

We can't change the future, but we can prepare to receive it. Like cultivating the garden before planting, we prepare the ground to receive its seed, the potential of new life. And that is what the future brings, this vast and endless potential, all that is yet to be. If you will look toward the future, it can re-shape the present. In fact, we can become like the future before it arrives. How?

One of the gifts that great seers provide is a compelling vision of the future. Poets and prophets cast visions of a future that has yet to materialize, a world not seen with the eyes but rather with the hopeful imagination of what could be. They describe a peaceable kingdom that does not yet exist. They announce healing before it arrives. As they do, and as we imagine it, we become more able to transform ourselves in the image of that vision. When we are captured by a future vision, we become more like that which we imagine.

The future, however, is never entirely as we imagine it. There are too many unseen variables, too many simultaneous acting forces for us to predict or know the outcomes. So though we shape the impact of the future through preparation and imagination, the future still remains wild and uncontrollable. That is the challenge and fulfillment of the future for us; it does and does not meet our expectations.

Since we do and do not affect the future by how we view and prepare for it, blessing comes in both earned and unearned form. Some things materialize in the present because we will them so; we prepare for and foster certain outcomes. If we believe in a vision, it often comes to pass. At the same time, other people, events, and circumstances arrive unexpectedly, not at all as the result of our planning or effort. Any arrival of the future bears these unexpected contents that are disconnected from the causes and effects of which we are aware. This includes everything from suffering to surprising opportunities that come our way.

Whereas the sign over the back door reads "remember," the sign above the front door reads "hope." Most importantly, the future door opens to hope. With hope we may take another step beyond despair, believing in that which is not yet seen. Hope embraces a power of the future that is able to transform the present. The future is not just a delivery truck that arrives at your door and leaves a package; it is the truck of potential that may liberate us from the tyranny of the present moment and deliver us to somewhere else.

Our fundamental apprehension about the future is related to the fear of death, our anxiety about non-being. Our big-brained human consciousness includes an awareness of death, one that expands and becomes clearer the longer we live and the closer our end becomes.

Second-tier fears often derive from the quintessential dread that our time is short and we will inevitably come to an end.

So, for example, fear during illness is often related to a suspicion that illness will worsen and lead to death. Suffering and pain are reminders that we are finite and mortal, that we have a brief shelf life and are not invincible. Our fear of scarcity, that we will not have enough of the basics, is directly related to the fact that without enough we will not survive. The normal signs of our aging and the aging of those around us restate the unavoidable, that all is passing way and nothing is permanent, including us.

However we mask or distract ourselves from mortality, its reality remains undeniable. If we are afraid the future will demonstrate that life is meaningless, we are even more afraid that we will not even exist to discover that. Our fear of the future arises from our fear of death.

Most people do not deal with the fear of death through behavioral adjustments, relaxation exercises, or cognitive therapy. They find the answer instead through philosophical or spiritual pathways; one's life must be understood from a different vantage point. Whether this understanding comes from embracing the new physics and its enlarged cosmology, or from ancient religious traditions that describe pathways to transcendence, the self is placed in relationship to a much larger context of meaning. To access that, we will pass through the door to the attic, a threshold we have yet to cross. Until then, however, we recognize that our apprehension about the future is related to our mortality.

If your reservoir is low on hope and high on fear, now is the time to exchange those two. Hope is a sacred gift that has the power to displace fear, anxiety, and dread. Hope is the conviction that the same power and presence of the universe that *has* sustained you up until now *will be* sustaining you in everything yet to come. Whereas fear focuses on the worst that can be, anything that might inflict pain or cruel scarcity upon us, hope attends to the opposite. Hope embraces the beautiful, creative, loving, and new that comes our way. Hope is on the lookout for all these things, watching and waiting with expectancy. And because hope is on the lookout for these things, it often notices them when they appear. Above all, a hopeful person is an attentive person, noticing all the blessings which surround us and are arriving all the time.

Throughout the history of the two-legged, big-brained creatures, hope has often been the single most important factor that determined surviving rather than perishing. Without hope, people cave in, roll over, and die. With it, entire new chapters of the grand story emerge. You will, as you look out this door, need to make a decision. Which kind of person will you be? Defined by hope or not?

One of the remarkable things about life is the way that all actions of our present moment generate waves of influence that move ahead of us and wait in the future. Many things we say or do today hold consequences that will materialize years from now. And we will discover them through remarkable and unexpected pathways, frequently in different forms than they began.

That is why so many artists, creators, and innovators launch their work into the world only to find it is before its time; the gift must wait for a different time, circumstance, and audience in order to be received by those who are ready. That is why we must entrust our lives to the mysterious unfolding future. We may not see the fruit of our labor now, or ever, but someone, somewhere will. Hoping and trusting releases and receives the gifts of the universe. These gifts manifest themselves in their own time and way. A million variables will align and intersect to create a new and surprising outcome.

Front Door

At times parents wonder whether anything they say or do matters to their children, whether their actions or words make a real difference. As hard as they try, they cannot see the fruits of their labor. But later, whether years or decades, they find the trace, the string to the past, the one foundation stone upon which the most dynamic aspect has arisen. And like time travelers, they connect the dots between what happened long ago with a secret unfolding. Hope knows that the future safeguards those treasures for just the right moment.

When peacemakers go about their work of reconciliation, the results so often seem insignificant. The behavior of the affected parties seems to change so very little. Later, however, the work of the peacemaker often shows itself, the slumbering seed germinating within the heart of someone, some group. Suddenly the memory of what was experienced earlier unites with present reality and a new pathway opens. This happens months, years, and even decades later. The action of the present travels to the future and waits on new arrivals.

Now the hard or joyful work begins. If you take courage, refuse to flee, and instead face what shows itself, you may claim your transformed life. In order to do so, certain practices are necessary, practices that are absolutely essential for navigating the other side of the door. Now spend time with each one:

Anticipate the future in order to transform the present.
Exchange anxiety for excitement.
Remember that fear arises just before your greatest breakthroughs.
Let go of your attempt to control every aspect of the future.
Receive the arrival of each day as a gift.
Be willing to let go in order to pick up.
Adapt to the new agenda the future provides.
Allow hope to define the way you are.

Now with the front door opened wide and the back door left standing ajar, look across the house from back door to front door. There is a clear sight line between the past and the future, a kind of time line that runs right through your house. You are standing in the middle of it. Feel yourself in the flux of time.

Six Doors to the Seventh Dimension

    As you stand at that intersection between front door and back door and the two side doors, you simultaneously experience the movement of time and the connection of nature with humanity. From that one vantage point you become aware of a pulse in the fabric of time and space.

    When you are ready, follow me to the next door. Feel free to rest in your special chair on the way. This is hard work.

Front Door

Excursus

Dare we trust this door?

The unknown future blesses the present moment. We release the ink, making our picture. We soak the page with our life force. I am here now, we tell the future. This is the time of my heart.

Hand on my chest, I can't count the future heartbeats inside. They are immeasurable. I have to feel them one by one.

I hope I have many still to come—strong beats that mean something to the one who cares enough to listen, head on my chest.

If hope were clothing, how would it feel? In winter, it would be a ribbed sweater, enough weight to feel substantial, enough stretch to feel cozy, keeping you warm when it's mean and cold out.

In summer, it would be a gauzy, honey-colored sarong, wrapped around a bathing suit for a walk down the beach. Loose enough to catch the sea breeze, it would keep you cool when it's hot out, protecting you from too much sun.

It feels good to live in hope, comfortable and energizing. It looks attractive on every person; it suits all of us. Why then, do we still have fear about the future? A sense of doom or impending ruin. Inevitable loneliness or worsening health. A run-of-the-mill weariness about coming days. Fear in different flavors, all of them bitter and gritty with a filmy aftertaste.

Sometimes I forget the future can be full of kindness. It might offer me animal crackers—the taste of innocence. The future might be an afternoon nap under an umbrella, as I snooze to the happy sounds of children building sandcastles nearby. The waves whoosh in and pull out.

Sunset comes. Friends gather around a bonfire on the beach. Someone plays a guitar.

Six Doors to the Seventh Dimension

How to live as context, not self? I want to live as a guitar, not a string. My time to break will come. I will be replaced. But today, I vibrate. I'm part of a song around a bonfire at the beach.

In the future, it is a reunion of friends. We are all there, together.

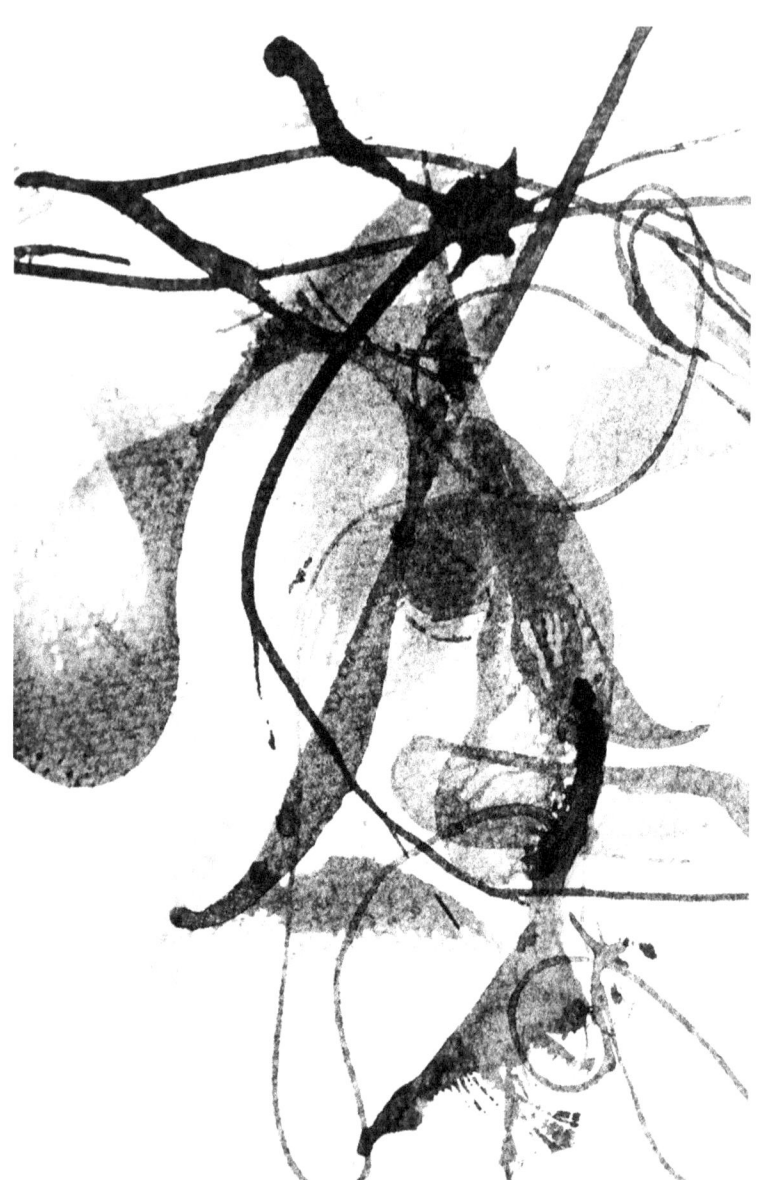

Chapter 5

Basement Door

We connect with our basement and its forces to stand against adversity, pursue what is important, seek satisfaction, and stoke our creativity. It is always honest about what it wants and what it has to give. And we may borrow its energy for great purposes, everything from saving and protecting the weak, to creating great works of art, to pursuing our heart's desire. This is the source of the house's energy grid, the unfiltered primal energy.

When we ignore the power of the basement, we partition our native instincts and drives. When we ignore the power of the basement, our creative energy goes unused and often stagnates. When we ignore the power of the basement, we feel disempowered in the face of threat, conflict, and challenge. And because this basement energy is so often affiliated with the body, we often become afraid of it and mistrust it. The basement energy contains a deeply emotional, embodied, and often irrational wisdom that may be unsettling.

When you are ready, take a deep breath, turn the doorknob, and open the door.

When you pass through this threshold, you immediately begin to descend the basement stairs. The light switch is on the right side just inside the door. Wait a moment for your eyes to adjust to the dim light. Each step takes you downward toward aspects of your life that have been partially hidden. But just because they are out of view, it does not mean they are inactive. To the contrary, they are alive and well, operating in subtle ways all the time. In fact, the more hidden they are, the more control they exert from the shadows, from offstage. It is time to get better acquainted.

As you descend, you may notice your logical, rational mind releasing its grip. The part of you accustomed to calculating, analyzing, and evaluating quiets as the upstairs disappears into the background. Now you begin to sense another kind of energy, the basement energy, unregulated emotional energy, and it is free-flowing, raw, and basic. You have now entered the place of instinct, desire, survival, power, intuition, and creativity. You actually feel the basement more than you think about it.

This is your inner kennel, the place where you experience the raw instinct and drive of fellow creatures to feed, defend, and procreate. Within this archaic layer lives your instinctual self, your body wisdom that knows what it knows before you think it. This locale makes instant decisions about threats, sexual satisfaction, pleasure, and sensation. The basement is where you want, need, pursue, protect, and create. Many of your most original, passionate, imaginative, urgent, and honest responses originate from this realm. It is from here that you hunt the prey, build the fire, and cook and eat your meal. It is here that you build protective shelter and create weapons to defend against threats to your security. Somewhere in these shadows, you exert your impulse to power. Whereas Dr. Jekyll lives on the main floor of your house, Mr. Hyde lives in your basement. But there are more characters living here.

In the far corner, Conan the Barbarian and Xena the Warrior Princess sharpen their swords and practice for combat. Across from the warriors are the lovers, Romeo and Juliet, talking over the exploits of Don Juan and thumbing through their well-worn copy of the Kama Sutra. Just beyond two easels sit Georgia O'Keefe and Pablo Picasso discussing color, brush strokes, and new ways of expression. In the center of the basement sits the Great Mother, extending her engorged breast to the hungry baby to suckle.

Basement Door

They are all there. Get to know them one by one. After all, this coterie is an important part of you, the cast and characters of the basement that make up much of what you are. If you refuse to regard and recognize them, they will gain your attention in their own ways.

Because the instinctual energy affiliated with the basement realm is so very native and unfiltered, it often lives in tension with the other rooms of your house, rooms holding competing convictions as to what is good and right for you and others. Negotiating that tension between the desires of the basement and convictions of the other rooms is one of the great challenges of life.

One way to deal with this tension is to ignore or silence the voices from the basement. That usually does not work well, or work for long, because it does not go away; it only goes underground. There, out of sight and out of conscious mind, its force continues to exert its influence on the rest of the house, often backing up in the plumbing and overflowing into the floors above.

That is precisely why we must go to the basement and spend time there. The basement must become a familiar place where we are acquainted with and befriend the cast of characters that inhabits it. It is only when we know them by name that they become part of the rest of the house. Then, and only then will the power of the basement be put at the disposal of the rest of the house and become a source of pure energy.

Whereas other rooms of the house may provide a more complex moral compass, this domain, the basement, supplies the raw stuff that allows us to decide quickly, act decisively, and pursue single-mindedly. It operates by its own rules. When we are disconnected from the basement, we often become timid in the world, separated from our own power.

Caution is due as well. If the basement energies remain untempered by other aspects of the house, they may become ruthless, selfish, and insensitive to the needs of others. The basement needs relationship with all other aspects of the house, just as those other aspects need living connection with it.

Six Doors to the Seventh Dimension

Now the hard or joyful work begins. If you take courage, refuse to flee, and instead face what shows itself, you may claim your transformed life. In order to do so, certain practices are necessary, practices that are absolutely essential for navigating the other side of the door. Now spend time with each one:

> Recognize the pulsing power beneath your own feet.
> Listen to the voice of your own deep energy.
> Invite those powers into your awareness.
> Liberate that rich desire to energize daily life.
> Borrow instinctual energy for noble efforts.
> Unleash the power of all your subterranean characters.

There is an opening on the floor beside the Great Mother that reveals a descending circular staircase, a vertical labyrinth, and at the bottom of the shaft an open space, and in the open space all manner of young animals resting, playing, and speaking. These are the inhabitants of your inner jungle cave. Some are domesticated and others not. They all know you, belong to you, long for you. And though you may worry that they bite, they will not; in fact, they are only provoked when ignored.

Now sit among them. Watch and listen. Hold them in your lap. Feel their breathing and movement. Sense what they know. Love them and receive their attention. You are holding powerful aspects of yourself.

When you are ready, follow me to the next door. Feel free to rest in your special chair on the way. This is hard work.

Excursus

The basement is a place of underground rumors and full body shakes.

Fight. Eat. Breed.

Fist. Mouth. Womb.

The basement is a place of the primitive, home of our ancient natures.

On the main floor, we had a neat fire in the fireplace. The chimney was inspected at regular intervals. The contained fire is started with split wood and crumbled newspapers. It is a fire where we sit, read, and rest.

In the basement, we burn branches found on a virgin forest floor, piled high to burn under as many stars as there are shark teeth at the bottom of the sea. It's the fire started from sparks, rapid hands, and desire. Will this fire take over everything if we let it? Will it go wild? We circle the heat in bare feet, chanting and dancing as a group, shadows taller than bodies blending into the night.

The basement is a place of denied reflections and untamable appetites.

We have the way we are used to looking at things, the way we expect, the way we are most comfortable. We look at mirrors face forward.

Every once in a while, we look at our backside with a mirror.

How often do we stand on a mirror and look down from this angle? The basement is the view from below.

Young animals tussle and scuffle. I took a few and tried to wash them. They smelled like animals. I tried to train them, and raise them up in civilized ways.

Yet there were always more raw, rough, young animals than I could domesticate. How then will I make peace with such difficult creatures, creatures with no interest in clothes, peace, or cleanliness?

In retreat to this dark den, I can take notice of the creatures. The attention won't tame them, but it does calm them.

They didn't want to be invisible. Doesn't everyone want to be seen?

Here we see them, and we see ourselves.

We see our base selves.

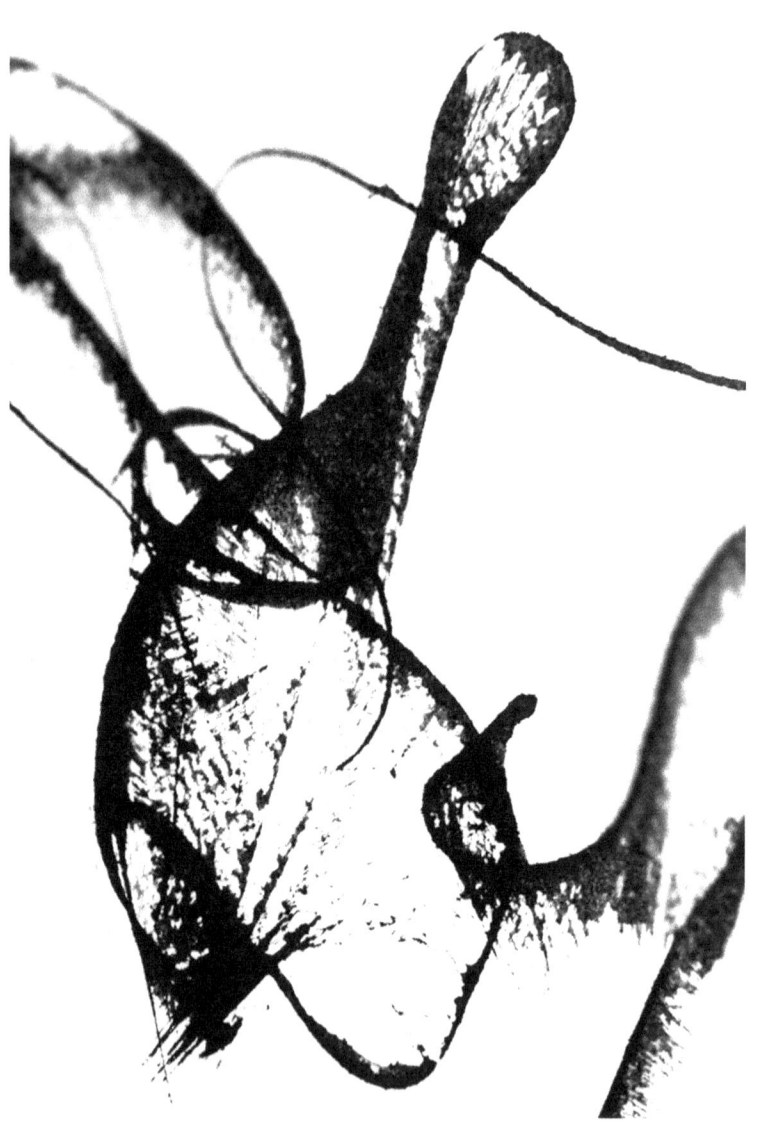

Chapter 6

Attic Door

The first thing you notice about the attic door is its unique position. Obviously you have to climb up the stairs to approach it, and the change in altitude itself means something. This is going to be a different kind of move, something that contrasts with the five doors that preceded it.

In the same way that you can see farther and differently on the top of a mountain, so you may see differently in the attic of your house. You are approaching a domain where perspective may change, and you yourself may change. You know things up here differently. Business as usual doesn't apply.

When you are ready, take a deep breath, climb the ladder, and open the door.

As you pass through the threshold into the attic, you immediately notice how spacious it is. Viewed from the outside, such enormous interior spans seem impossible. On the inside, however, the space is cavernous, like the inside of a large warehouse, or cathedral, or public building. The space is filled with levels, staircases, and platforms that overlook the huge central atrium. An interior stroll takes you up and through these different levels, each one visible to the next. It remains entirely unclear where one plane ends and the next begins. It is space composed of undefined edges, if you can call them edges at all.

Just after looking into the attic space, you hear its sounds. They are familiar sounds because they underlie every other sound you have ever heard. These sounds are not music in the customary sense of the word. But the vibration and harmonies resonate with our bodies and minds. We hear the sound without knowing its origin. In the same way, the attic is lighted, but not from a discernable source; it is filled with light.

The attic is dream-like and dream-filled. This dreamscape includes incense, candles, robed figures conducting mysterious rituals, religious art, mystics in prayer, universal symbols, myths, and stories, non-rational speech, and luminaries of the great spiritual traditions.

In the same way that you stand in the continuums of past-future and nature-humanity, so the open door to the basement and the open door to the attic create a spectrum of under and over forces, the basement and attic energies balancing and completing one another.

One of the functions of the attic is to provide you with your own highest humanity: superlative moral codes, vast compassion, and a way of life that is filled with faith, hope, and love. The attic expands perspective and enlarges our concern for neighbor. And it is there we find our great moral and spiritual teachers.

The attic is that liminal space between our house and what lies beyond it. Think of the attic as an antechamber to a larger reality we have yet to explore. Every religious expression is a human response to the infinite mystery of the universe. It is to this infinite dimension that religious traditions point by whatever finite means they can. And every authentic religious community knows the difference between their pointing and what it is they point to.

If the house of your life took the form of your body, you would feel its energy coursing from the top to the bottom of you. As it rose as high as your forehead, the attic level, you would sense a higher awareness, what we call a spiritual sensibility, a doorway to an enriched consciousness that is connected to, informs, and enriches every other doorway. In the attic you stand at the edge of

Attic Door

infinity without having crossed over into it. It, however, starts to cross over into you.

After you enter the attic, you become aware that if there are any blockages in the rest of the house, they will impede the free flow of energy through your entire system. Identifying and naming those blocks and finding ways to release them returns the flow of spirit from top to bottom, every floor to every room. The converse is true as well; once you draw on the energy of the attic space, it tends to unstick every other place in the house.

It is interesting that when Jesus tells the seeker Nicodemus (John 3:3) that to enter the realm of God he must be born *anothen* (Gk), the ancient word may be translated several ways into modern English. The most familiar traditional rendering is *again*—you must be born again. But just as easily, the Greek word means *anew* or *from above*. You must be born from above.

In one way or another, said Jesus, you must go up to the attic, draw on its power, and be born from above. There you will find a spacious view of everything else. And most importantly you will begin to prepare for a possibility you could scarcely imagine before, that of the arriving and already present realm of God.

Every spiritual tradition, including the Christian one, carries time-honored spiritual practices that take people toward the mystery of God. None of these practices magically propel people into the great mystery apart from faith. Without the participation of heart, body, and mind they cannot. But the traditions, practices, and rituals prepare the willing soul to receive the Absolute, Infinite or Eternal.

Christians, for example, read sacred texts, pray alone and together, practice charity, keep silence, engage in the sacramental drama of Holy Communion, and sing poetic sacred verse. All of this prepares them for the experience of God, something beyond simple comprehension. When Christians recite The Lord's Prayer with heart and say "Our Father, who is in heaven, holy is your name . . .," they open themselves to the hidden God who cannot be seen, the sacred presence of the universe, in hopes of finding communion and even union with that presence. The prayer is not God, but prepares the heart to embrace God.

Now the hard or joyful work begins. If you take courage, refuse to flee, and instead face what shows itself, you may claim your transformed life. In order to do so, certain practices are necessary, practices that are absolutely essential for navigating the other side of the door. Now spend time with each one:

> Open your heart to the universal truths that last.
> Embrace the higher attributes of faith, hope, and love.
> Suspend your pre-existing certainty.
> Engage in spiritual practices that prepare you for more.
> Seek truth in both the seen and unseen.

If you will stand on the main floor in the center of the house, you will find yourself located in the confluence of many forces. The intersections where past-future, nature-humanity, and basement-attic meet comprise a kind of portal, an entrée to something beyond them. This is the intersection of the six doors, an intersection where the thin space of the attic ushers you toward the seventh dimension. But not even the attic, the sixth door, can take you there. It only positions you to go there.

No mythology, symbol system, ritual, religious path, or spiritual leader can do that. They can open channels, point you, prepare you, lead you, and go with you. But the next and essential step must be yours, the step toward the infinite power to which you belong.

For this reason I can go no farther with you. We have arrived at the end of my ability to serve as your guide. From here on, this journey belongs to you and you alone. Beyond this threshold you must travel solo, alone except for the unseen power and energy that beckons all of us forward.

Many people have stopped right here where you are now standing, at the intersection of the six doors. They have all realized greater happiness and contentment as a result of their integration of the many aspects of the six doors. So if you are not able to travel any farther, or travel farther now, be reassured that your journey has not been in vain; you have dared to draw together the many aspects accessible to this dimension of life.

The next step beyond the everyday main floor of your house, beyond our perception of time that holds a past and a future, beyond matter and its manifestations in the world of nature and humans, beyond deep layers of instinct and the highest aspirations of spirit, will take you beneath the surface of appearance and beyond cause and effect physics. The next leg of your journey requires a leap of imagination and what many have called faith.

I leave you with this one clue: It was from the attic that Jesus said his Father's house has many rooms and that he travels on ahead to prepare a place. You have already explored the worlds behind your many doors. Now he points toward something beyond, as though your house is but one room of a more expansive reality. Your normal operating procedures will become irrelevant. You will need to suspend assumptions about the way things are and how to navigate. It is time to reach beyond the apparent. What is required is no less than a transformation of your seeing, awareness, and consciousness. Not everyone has been able to travel here, in this way. I hope you are called to do so.

Six Doors to the Seventh Dimension

Excursus

Most of our life, we knew our place and defined it with directions. North, or 150 miles from St. Louis, or in the living room. We contained ourselves inside our personal set of recognizable landmarks. We oriented ourselves with the sun.

In this new place, we find no recognizable round disc to help us track time and shadows. We float in the idea of heaven. Not heaven itself, but the hint of it.

We hear a comforting murmur of prayers repeated in unison by the holy ones. In harmony with their prayers, we sense music that has the quality of being remembered more than heard.

We glide, glistening, unrestricted by the weight of bones. Earth's gravity holds less sway here.

Pre-existing calamity is gone from our minds.

They say it is not easy to be born. The birth process smushes and reshapes us. It takes a while for our heads to come back to their natural shape.

This is the room—the place of the second birth—that can most reshape us.

Yet I struggle to reconcile my earthbound body with such a room.

Considering this attic world is like describing the sky to a blind mole rat. I say, "There is a sky above this thick clay. It is all air. As evening falls, the clear air is transparent. Stars light-years away make pinpricks of brightness in the dark stretch of night fabric. In day, the color of peace—blue—stretches wide enough for three thousand white clouds to meander through, yet there is still more blue. And I haven't even started to tell you about the aurora borealis!"

My mole self answers, "I know clay, roots and digging tunnels. The feel of ground giving way from my teeth and the scent of fresh earth as it's broken open. Why be so

Attic Door

unanchored, to climb thin bars of a ladder, to prepare for dissolving into illumination. Is the snugness of this tunnel not peace enough? Is seeking more roots to chew not faith enough?"

"No, mole self," I say. "We must climb. Love calls."

Hands on the ladder, we climb.

The Seventh Dimension

When I looked down at my feet, I saw that they were positioned at the great confluence of the doors, the intersections of past and future, nature and humanity, subterranean forces and transcendent aspirations. This was the expansive view provided by the doors. I felt the energy surge up and down every connected facet of my being.

This new awareness allowed me to let go, surrender control, and look on myself and my surroundings in a new way, with a kind of detached curiosity. I was a self and had a self at the same time. I was in the picture and looking at it from a distance. This new perception of what was before me had a peculiar paradoxical effect: as each object presented itself, it assumed a gauze-like and transparent visage. I was standing at the edge of some unexplainable union, the connection of all elements above and below, but I was not sure how. I began to feel one with everything I did not understand. It was an edge I occupied, an edge between my finite world and a new, infinite one.

And then I knew it was necessary to let go of every part of myself that was not worthy of the mystery, every inferior thing that could not survive in the realm of light, every weight and encumbrance that imprisoned my spirit. Without that surrender I would automatically boomerang back to the finite world of sense to which I was so strongly attached.

I looked and saw that the substantial nature of the house was dissolving, and what had seemed so permanent was becoming more and more fluid. I turned and gazed upward and watched in amazement as the roof began to separate at the peak, split and peel back, all four walls moving apart with it. Slowly, smoothly, the walls tilted out and away from the center, tipping toward the outside in four directions. They fell outward until they lay flat, joining with the floor to create one plane upon which I stood, a huge floor that now extended endlessly in all directions.

Then I saw that there were no more walls, and without walls, no doors. Without doors, there were no thresholds that opened to distinct realities. The changing form of the house revealed what had been hidden all along, a seamless field of energy. Once the finite boundaries dissolved, I saw how external form had concealed the underlying powers.

Our walls were ever before us. We were the wallmakers, the joiners of corners and the hingers of doors. We wanted walls to define space. A small space made us feel bigger. We needed flat definitions until the moment came when we didn't. We let the walls open and became our true size.

ALL IS ONE.

Then I looked at the pure radiance and realized that it had always filled the ordinary chambers of the house by different degree; each aspect, each door and threshold revealed more and different light. The hidden energy always found its way to the ordinary surface of life, a manifestation of the power and majesty that animated all things. What was hidden showed itself in what was seen. The world was filled to the brim with its sacred contents. Supernal light filtered into the hearts of great spiritual souls who guided others to what they had glimpsed themselves. But then I caught a glimpse of even more, an original harmony and beauty, the highest realities unsullied by the lowest.

As I stepped toward this original harmony, I let go of all the dualistic ways I previously viewed life. I saw that past, present, and future were not absolute realities, but only perceptions of my own mind, ways of understanding shaped by my own limits. I suddenly realized that the passage of time is something experienced by those who live within the walls. Once the walls of the house flattened and became a part of that one plane, I began to fall toward timelessness, the fullness of time, looking and listening through the waterfall of eternity.

We made walls on paper and called it a calendar. A day was a box with a number. We needed to measure our existence using time until the moment came when we didn't. Without walls on the calendar—boxes to make us feel bigger—we become pure presence. We listen to the water.

All is one,

one always.

When the walls and their doors finally disappeared, the differences between me and every other creature were revealed for what they were: different manifestations of the same spirit energy. Almost every difference had to do with outer form, the ways particular things had changed and transformed in time and space. At the root, though, the source, spirit, and energy that infused all, remained identical.

Though much of this seemed inconceivable to me, the more I stepped toward the great mystery, the more I began to notice the unity of those things that used to appear as opposites. Back when the walls were all in place, only doorways allowed for connections between realms. I realized that all these infinite connections had always been there. If my journey had begun with doorways revealing interconnected aspects, it concluded with the façade of the house peeling away to reveal what stood behind it all along.

The sixth door ushered me to the edge of the seventh dimension, its antechamber and threshold, but not into it. As I moved forward, I had to let go of everything that brought me to the edge of the mystery. I was overcome by a fearsome wonder as I came face to face with the infinitely complex, endless, and indefinite. The closer I was, the smaller I felt. The smaller I felt, the less I attempted to control anything. The less I attempted to control, the more I collapsed into pure wonder.

We used to think of our skin as a kind of wall. This is the edge of me. I can go no further. We needed to keep ourselves separate until the moment came when we didn't. Then skin became a tender place of communication and exchange, not separation.

Our energy concentrates in different ways. The glint of a star: ours. The plight of a penguin: ours. The expanse of space: ours. The freeform flow of an amoeba: ours. All the same starting material, all the same end point, and all the same elements in between.

ALL IS ONE,

ONE ALWAYS,

ALWAYS EVERYWHERE.

The six doors provided healing, thankful memory, connection with nature and humans, hope, instinctual depth, and pathways toward a higher, greater self. All of these combined together to create balance, harmony, purpose, and wisdom. The main floor had been transformed into a richly variegated tapestry of life. But here, beyond the six doors, was yet another dimension, a seventh dimension that both fulfilled and transformed all that preceded it.

Here was completeness and perfection, the spiritual essence and elegance of life. This multi-layered journey had taken me through a veritable geography of the spirit. But then I was faced with taking another step, a mystical one, forgetting myself as I joined with absolute being, pure light, and the original energy. The most important determining forces of the universe were not found in what was seen, but rather what was unseen; not in the apparent, but in the counter-intuitive.

We used to want to make a name for ourselves. Making a name and living up to a name took a lot of effort. And we kept naming things until the moment came when we didn't. Peace doesn't need a name. It is. Always it holds us, the way an old friend wraps her arms around you and puts her hand on your heart. All is forgiven. All is given. We stay together.

ALL IS ONE,

ONE ALWAYS,

ALWAYS EVERYWHERE,

EVERYWHERE ALL.

The plane into which I had fallen was an infinite one; extending endlessly in space and indefinitely in time, at least as far as I could imagine. What I was able to imagine, however, was relatively little. These infinities were inconceivable with my finite mind, limited by my assumptions and perceptions. I began to let go.

And then I looked and realized that the infinite plane of which I was a part belonged to a greater infinity. The complexity was immense, all my former categories irrelevant, and the illusion of predictable boundaries passing away. Language failed me. What do the words *more* and *less* really mean when spoken against the background of infinity? If time and space are relative, what exactly do the words *near* and *far* mean? I first ran out of words, then numbers, and finally concepts and explanations for how things work. There would be no explanations for infinity by finite means.

All the forms of finite existence that shaped my understanding were actually a part of an infinite cosmos, a seamless garment. It was what religious figures and great philosophers had glimpsed for thousands of years in thousands of places. The strange world of quantum physics had identified the same underlying realities that these mystics had known intuitively and named differently.

    When I looked again at the plane upon which I was standing, how it extended unendingly in all directions at once, I finally saw that it is only one of many planes above and below, infinitely many planes, layered even as they are connected. I realized this not with senses or an analytical brain, but instead with my mind, a mind merged with the greater Mind of the world. In that moment of clarity, my location, whether within one plane or many, vanished. There arose a great, full emptiness. The emptiness flooded with radiance. And then, finally, something enveloped me, something good, pure and loving, the unified, infinite, and energy-filled hum of the universe.

A long time ago—the time before words—we knew a heartbeat. As time passed, we learned to worry. Then the moment finally came when we didn't. Without numbers, the calendars faded in the light. Our reason put on a fierce resistance. In our own heads, our ideas seemed large. Yet we surrendered, gave them away. Our old ideas look like tiny seed pod boats swirling along a rushing spring creek. Why were we ever attached to those? We live by the heartbeat again. We enter the great idea from the Mind whose wisdom we've been seeking. From our toes to our head, our starlight to our penguin, we gleam.

ALL IS ONE,

ONE ALWAYS,

ALWAYS EVERYWHERE,

EVERYWHERE ALL,

ALL IS ONE.

About the Creators

Timothy Carson is a pastor and writer who enjoys the arts, travel, and sharing intimate times with friends and family. When he is not pastoring or writing about culturally relevant spirituality, you can find him reading, playing with raptors, and exploring the history of his beloved central Missouri. You can keep up with him through vitalwholeness.wordpress.com.

Jenny McGee is a professional artist who is passionate about helping people express themselves through her abstract paintings. Jenny considers herself a work in progress and is still waiting to grow taller. She is a cancer survivor who is learning to love her freckles and life's imperfections, and cherishes each moment with her husband, David, and two children, Jonny and Ema Blue. You can learn more, express, and celebrate with Jenny at www.jennymcgeeart.com.

Genevieve A. Howard is a writer and communication professional who loves ponies, prayer, tea, and hugs. She lives in a country home, performing stunts with yarn and attending to the needs of her half-dozen animals. She loves to spend lazy afternoons with her husband, son, and friends, with a cup of tea, of course. Connect with her at genevievehoward.com.

www.ingramcontent.com/pod-product-compliance
Lightning Source LLC
Chambersburg PA
CBHW070101100426
42743CB00012B/2619